Raspberry Pi

A Beginner's Guide to

Raspberry Pi Programming

Table of Contents

Introduction

Are you looking for a way to learn how to code, but that doesn't require shelling out hundreds of dollars for a computer or getting tangled in a lengthy setup? If you answered yes, then Raspberry Pi could be the answer for you!

Raspberry Pi made its debut on February 24th, 2012. Unfortunately, the website of the original supplying firm crashed. However, new models of Raspberry Pi 2 have been released and are currently in circulation.

This device is a global phenomenon. It is useful for various activities, such as being a regulator for smart home appliances and acting as a media center. Additionally, Raspberry Pi can serve as a desktop workstation, and using it, beginners can learn to code or decode the Python programming language.

You can begin to write programs for your device using the renowned Python programming language and learn the essentials of graphical user interfaces. Understanding the pygame module will also assist you in building fun and exciting games.

In this book, you will learn the ABCs of Raspberry Pi, from setting it up, to writing your first lines of code, to creating fun and interesting projects.

Let's dive in to learn more!

Chapter One: Understanding Raspberry Pi

What Is a Raspberry Pi?

If you take a look at the structure of a Raspberry Pi, the first thing you'll notice is how small it is. The size of a Raspberry Pi is similar to that of a typical credit card. This small form is itself a characteristic feature of the device, although it may not look entirely like a final product straight out of the box.

Raspberry Pi functions as a desktop computer designed to access the internet and play games. It can help you to build spreadsheets, word-processing documents, and even to play high-definition videos.

This device can help beginners and experienced software engineers to learn computing skills and programming languages such as Python and Scratch. A Pi is an affordable computer device you can fit in the palm of your hand, and that you can plug into a television or computer monitor. It also functions with a mouse and a standard keyboard.

The birth of Raspberry Pi was inspired by the notion that fully functioning computers in a compact size, made available to the general consumer at a reasonable price, would hold enough power to not only facilitate the educational industry, but also make computer technology easier to implement and customize in various projects (for example, educational projects, DIY projects, or any experiment that can use the prowess of the Raspberry Pi). The Raspberry Pi Foundation was established in 2012, and after a limited production of units, the beta testing became a huge success. Today, Raspberry Pi has taken a strong foothold in various human interactive environments, including homes, offices, smart factories, data centers, interactive classrooms, and other such places which can take advantage of the features of a small handheld computer.

Different Models of Raspberry Pi

There are numerous different models of the Raspberry Pi. Since the market launch in 2012, the performance of the minicomputers has developed significantly. The following versions of the Raspberry Pi are among the best known:

- Raspberry Pi 4 B

- Raspberry Pi 3 Model A+

- Raspberry Pi 3B+

- Raspberry Pi Zero WH

- Raspberry Pi Zero W

- Raspberry Pi 3 Model B

- Raspberry Pi 2 Model B

- Raspberry Pi Zero

- Raspberry Pi 1 Model B and B+

- Raspberry Pi 1 Model A and A+

Since the release of the first Raspberry Pi Model A, many models have followed, each of them bringing improved functionality and specifications in general. Hence, before you go out and get yourself a Raspberry Pi, be sure that you know which model you are purchasing and whether it suits your needs.

Despite the changes made in every model of the Raspberry Pi, there remains one aspect that has not been changed from the original Raspberry Pi A, and that is the software compatibility. This means that the software running on the original Raspberry Pi is the same software that's being used by the later versions; as such, the software being used in one Raspberry Pi is compatible with all other models, regardless of if they're newer or older. This is why the Raspberry Pi is so practical, because it focuses on usability and functionality above all else.

Just as how software developed for one Raspberry Pi model is compatible with the rest of the other models, all the different concepts and functions that we will learn in this book can be applied to any model in the Raspberry Pi family.

The Essential Features and Provisions of Raspberry Pi

Raspberry Pi exists in different generations, such as the Pi, P2, P3, and P4. These generations cost similarly to the first models but vary in the hardware and some features.

These latest technologies incorporate a board with a built-in Bluetooth feature. They are enabled by a Quad-Core Broadcom BCM283764bit ARMv8 processor. The P2 operates with 900 MHz, while the P3 functions at 1.2 GHz. All these models have four USB ports with a naked board that can be extended, including an upgraded power system.

The newer models of this device are designed with a built-in wireless connection. It features a hub with standard internet connectivity. Various gadgets can be interconnected to the device with flexible operational costs. Also, it works with a power source of 2.5 amps, so you do not need another cable to power more complex USB devices.

The General Provisions of Raspberry Pi

1. It has Bluetooth 4.1.

2. The video outputs include PAL and NTSC (composite video) using a 3.5 mm jack and HDMI.

3. It has four USB ports.

4. It has a CPU with Quad-core 64-bit ARM Cortex A53, reaching 1.2 GHz.

5. The device weighs 1.6 oz (45g).

6. The power source is 5 volts with a GPIO header or MicroUSB.

7. The size of the Raspberry Pi is 85.60 mm by 56.5 mm.

8. The memory has 1 GB LPDDR-900 SDRAM with Linux Operating System. That is 900 megahertz (MHz).

9. Raspbian has a network of 10/100 Mbps Ethernet and 802.IIn Wireless LAN.

10. The GPU has a 400-megahertz (MHz) Video core IV multimedia.

11. The peripherals are 17 GPIO with specific functions and a HAT ID bus.

12. Other specifications include a USB mouse and a USB Wi-Fi adapter.

The Specifications of the Hardware of Raspberry Pi

This microcomputer has the following specifications:

- **General Purpose Input & Output (GPIO) Pins**—You can interact with other electronic boards using the GPIO pins. Depending on the way you programmed your Raspberry Pi, these pins can receive and process input and output commands. It can function with digital GPIO pins too. Other electronic units are connected to the Raspbian through these pins. For instance, you can transmit digital data by connecting the general purpose input & output pins to the temperature sensor.

- **The Ethernet Port**—This port is designed for accessing the internet by plugging into your home router. It is the gateway for interacting with other devices.

- **Power Source Connector**—You can power your microcomputer using an external power source. This is a small switch beside the shield.

- **Central Processing Unit (CPU)**—The CPU works as the brain and hub of your system. It performs instructions on the computer using logical and mathematical functions. Raspberry Pi uses the ARM11 series processor, functioning with the same capacity of a Samsung Galaxy device.

- **Random Access Memory (RAM)**—If you compare Raspberry Pi to other computer devices, it is a miniature PC. Other standard computers have RAM measured in gigabytes, but the RAM of a Raspbian contains a minimum of 256 MB while the maximum RAM is 512 MB.

- **Display Monitors or TV**—Raspberry Pi board uses two types of monitors or television screens for displaying digital data. These include HDMI and Composite displays. Use a low-cost adaptor with an HDMI cable to connect with LCD and HD TV monitors. The versions of HDMI supported by your Raspberry Pi are 1.3 and 1.4 using 1.4 cables. However, it does not support the HDMI l/p adapter. The composite video functions are used for connecting old televisions. In this case, connecting the device to a display unit using a composite video connection can make the audio system functional. Connect the 3.5 mm jack socket and send it to your television.

- **Xbee Socket**—This feature in the board of a Raspberry Pi is used for wireless communication.

- **The Graphics Processing Unit (GPU)**—You can speed up the calculation of image functions using the GPU. This is a single chip on the board of your Raspberry Pi, and the GPU supports OpenGL. It is also built using a Broadcom video-core IV.

- **The Universal Asynchronous Receiver / Transmitter (UART)**—The UART is a serial input and output port used for transferring serial data like text. Programmers use it for debugging and converting codes.

Raspberry Pi has mass storage using an SD flash memory card. Your PC boots into Microsoft windows through the hard disk while an SD memory card helps the Raspbian to boot. Other specifications of the hardware include a US standard keyboard, video cable, power supply cable, monitor, and a microSD card with Linux operating system.

Other optional specifications you may need include a device case for model A or model B, a Wi-Fi adapter, an internet connection, a USB mouse, and a powered USB hub.

The Board of Raspberry Pi Model A

The board of model A is designed as a Broadcom (BCM2835) SOC board. This model is made with an ARM1176JZF-S Core CPU. It has an SD card of 256 MB RAM with 700 megahertz (MHz).

The USB 2.0 ports feature external data connectivity, which is an optional tool in the system. The board is powered through a micro-USB adapter. This adapter carries a minimum power range of 2 watts.

You can also speed up image calculation features using a graphics card, which is a special chip in the system. This feature is relevant for running a video or game through the Raspberry Pi.

The Features of the Board of Model A Raspberry Pi

The board of model A Raspberry Pi has unique features such as:

- The 2.0 USB connector is a single connection.

- The board has a dual-core video-core IV multimedia coprocessor.

- The dimensions of its board are 8.6 cm × 5.4 cm × 1.5 cm.

- The video output is composite featuring RCA (NTSC and PAL) and HDMI with cables versions 1.3 and 1.4.

- It comes with an audio output, a 3.5mm jack, and HDMI connection.

- Its board functions with an operating system called Linux.

- There is a slot for SD, SDIO, and MMC cards.

- The SD card RAM is 256 MB.

- It has a full HD multimedia processor with Broadcom BCM2835 SOC.

Chapter Two: Setting Up the Raspberry Pi

Now that we have some of the basics of the Raspberry Pi device down and we understand a few of the key features of the device, it is time for us to look a bit more at how we are actually able to use the device for our needs.

First, there will be a number of steps that we need to take to help us ensure that the Raspberry Pi will behave in the manner that we want and will complete all of the programs that we would like along the way as well.

It takes a little bit of time for us to set up this device and to make sure that it works the way that we need. The good news is that this will not be as complicated as it may seem.

In this chapter, we will look at getting started with the Raspberry Pi, including what components you will need, how to set up the operating system, and how to perform a test to ensure that our programs will run smoothly.

Let's dive in!

Things to Know to Get Started with Raspberry Pi

Before we can get started with this whole process, there will be a number of supplies that we need to purchase. To start, of course, we need to have the specific Raspberry Pi device that we would like. Some of the other supplies that we are able to work with when it comes to the Raspberry Pi device include:

- **A monitor or television that has an HDMI port**—You will need to be able to connect the device to some sort of display. A television or your computer monitor is fine as long as it can handle an HDMI connection. There are also some compact options that you can choose to work with if you wish.

- **A mouse and a keyboard**—These need to have a USB connection so that they can hook into the Raspberry Pi.

- **MicroSD card and its card reader**—The operating system that comes with the Raspberry Pi does not use a hard drive. Instead, it comes with a microSD card already installed. Make sure that you get one that has at least 8GB, or you won't be able to do much with the device. Your personal computer might have a card reader, so if you are using that, you are probably set.

- **Power supply**—The Raspberry device is powered through a micro-USB. This is similar to what your phone runs on. There are four USB ports to supply power. Just make sure that the power supply that you choose is able to give a minimum of 2.5A of power to the device.

These are just a few of the different parts that we are able to work with and are the most basic of what we are able to use. We are able to pick out other parts based on the project that we want to make. Once we have all of these parts nearby and ready to use, it is time to start the setup process and get the device to actually work.

How to Install the Operating System

To make use of the Raspberry Pi, we first need to make sure that the operating system is downloaded and ready. Without the operating system, we will only end up with a device that turns on but has a blank screen and nothing else. To install the operating system that we want, we first need to make sure that we have another regular computer to work with, either a desktop or a laptop.

The Raspbian operating system is the one that we will work with, but we first have to load it onto one of our regular computers and then use an SD card to tramsfer it over to the Pi device.

Now, you, as the programmer, will have a choice to make here, but I will limit it to two options. First, it is possible to go through and make sure that the operating system for Raspbian is manually installed on the system. This means that you have to bring in some external software to get this done, or you will have to know how to do so by typing in the command line. The second and the most common option that beginner programmers like to work with, is to use a NOOBS (New Out of the Box Software). These are easy to download and install, hence their appeal to beginners. Since this is the more favorable option for many people, we will look at the main steps that are necessary to make this happen below:

- First, we need to bring out the SD card that we would like to use for the card reader on the computer.

- Using our computer, we will spend a few minutes downloading the NOOBS.

There will be a few options for us to choose from. You can explore these options on the Raspbian website if you like, but to make it easier, we will choose the option for *offline and network install*. This is the option that will allow us to download the Raspbian operating system.

There are some situations where we need to do some formatting of our SD card as FAT (File Allocation Table). If this is the case with your card, then you are able to download this tool for formatting simply from the SD Association. From their website (sdcard.org), you need to look for the part that says *Format Size Adjustment*. Make sure that part is on in your options menu, and then your card will be all ready to go.

This is a process that will help us to end up with a good zip file to work with. You are then able to extract the operating system from here. When the extraction is done, make sure that you copy all of the contents of the folder to the SD card.

When this copying process is done, take the SD card from the card reader or the computer that you are using, and put it back into the Raspberry device. Now we have an SD card that has the Raspbian operating system on it, and that SD card should be on the Raspberry Pi device that we want to work with.

How to Hook Up the Raspberry Pi Device

Now that we have taken the time to work on downloading and installing our operating system, it is time for us to go through and ensure that each and every device that we will use with our Pi device can be hooked up and connected properly.

This will be a pretty simple step because you will just have to take on all of the parts and then plug them into the USB ports that are already found on the Raspberry Pi. However, you may find it best to do them in the following order.

The method we have below is the best to use because it will ensure that if you hook up a device to your Pi, that the Raspberry Pi will be able to recognize that device when it boots up. The most effective method of hooking things up to this device is to do so in the following order:

1. Start by connecting the monitor to the device.

2. When the monitor is recognized, you can connect the keyboard and the mouse as well.

3. If you want to work with an Ethernet cable in order to get your internet, then this is the time to connect it.

4. And finally, connect the power that you are using.

Since this device doesn't come with a power switch, as soon as that power source gets plugged into the device, then the device will turn on.

Setting Up Raspbian

At this point, we have had a chance to go through and get the operating system over to our SD card and are ready to go. But now, we need to make sure that we boot things up, especially the NOOBS that we talked about a bit earlier, so that we can use our device. This sometimes takes a few minutes, so you have to be prepared for nothing to happen right away. The reason for this is that the program of NOOBS takes a bit of time to format the SD card it is on and will do a check to make sure that the other parts are set up well. Keep this in mind, and don't get impatient with the speed here.

If you try to rush through all of this, or you skip ahead on it, this will risk corruption in the process, and your system will not work well. After the NOOBS program has had a few minutes to do the necessary tasks, you should notice on the Pi that there is a little screen that shows up. This screen will ask us to install the operating system that we would like to use on the device. You will be able to pick out any of the operating systems that you want here, but we will continue on with the steps to do Raspbian, as we talked about earlier. Some of the steps that we need to follow to make this happen include:

1. Look toward the bottom of your console screen. There should be a place there where you are able to select the keyboard layout, as well as the language, based on your region.

2. Look for the Raspbian operating system, and then check that box. This tells the system to install the operating system.

3. NOOBS will take on the work to install this operating system. This does take a little bit to complete, up to 20 minutes, so be patient.

When the Raspbian operating system is fully installed, you will be taken to the desktop for Raspbian, and you can then configure everything else that you need.

How to Configure the Raspberry Pi

When we get to this point, you should notice that the Raspberry Pi device is set up and ready to go. You should be able to look at the device and see your operating system, and there should also be a nice start menu for you to use. However, there are still a few other steps that we need to finish so that the Raspberry Pi device will work well, and we will begin with the *start menu.*

So, go to the start menu and click on it. You can then click on the section for *applications.*

Then click on the *file browser* to open it. This is where we are able to go through and enter any of the commands that you would like so that the system knows what it is supposed to do. This will be a similar process to other operating systems, and we will look at a few of the most common commands for this as we go.

There are a few other options that we need to look at when setting up the Raspberry Pi device before we get to those commands, however. We will look at some of these now, including how to install and set up the Bluetooth and Wi-Fi capabilities, so we can work on various projects and get the system to behave in the manner that we want in the long term.

Connecting the Raspberry Pi to Your Home Wi-Fi

You will be happy to know that it is pretty easy to connect the Raspberry Pi to your home Wi-Fi. In fact, you will be able to work with a lot of the same kinds of steps to hook up the Raspberry Pi to the internet as you would with one of your regular computers, whether it is your own laptop or a desktop computer. If you have done that in the past, then hooking up the Raspberry Pi device will be easy.

To start, look for the icon for *networks*, which should be found on the main menu of your Pi device. This will be a simple icon that just looks like there are two main computers that are right next to one another, and it should be somewhere on the top right corner of your screen.

When you are able to find that icon, click on it and then search for the Wi-Fi network that you would like to use. Click on the chosen network, enter the username and the password, and wait for it to connect. And that is really all there is to this process.

You have to make sure that you are using the right Wi-Fi and that you know the password and the username, but after a few moments of connecting, the Raspberry Pi device will have access to the internet.

Connecting to the Bluetooth Devices

In addition to hooking up your Raspberry Pi device to your home internet, it is time to learn how to connect the device over Bluetooth. There are many projects that make use of Bluetooth, so this is a good thing to set up at the beginning. This could be as simple as hooking up a keyboard or a mouse to the device so that you can use it more like a traditional computer, though this is not the only reason to set up a Bluetooth connection.

Setting this up will only take a few steps to accomplish. The first step is to go to your screen on the Pi and then check where the Bluetooth icon is located. Click on this icon, and then you can look for the option to *Add Device*.

Click there, and then go through all of the options that are presented to you there. Find the one device you would like to pair up with your device, and then follow the directions that show up on the screen. And that is really all there is to this whole process.

Just by going through and doing a simple search and clicking on the right icons along the way, you are able to enable Bluetooth on this device and get the Pi to work with any of the other Bluetooth-enabled devices that you own.

Once you can get these devices to sync up with one another, you are able to get them to work together, similar in the manner that you see on your regular computer.

Connecting to Raspberry Pi Remotely

The final thing that we will look at here is how we are able to hook up to our Raspberry Pi device in a remote manner. This is possible, and there are some situations where you may be doing some work on Raspberry Pi, and you notice that you need to get onto the device without a physical connection. Perhaps, at the time, you are not able to get the monitor near you to hook up, or you just need to work with that device when it is not sitting right next to you. This is something that we are able to do pretty easily when it comes to the Raspberry Pi. And we are able to use it just like we would with a regular computer, so the process is not too hard to understand and work with.

Some of the options that are at your disposal in order to connect remotely to the Raspberry Pi include:

- **Use the command line to connect:** You are able to use SSH from any computer in your home. This allows you to get a hold of the interface for command lines on the Raspberry Pi. While this option means that you can't access a graphic interface, you would instead be able to run any command that you want through the Terminal. When the command is sent through the Terminal, it will execute on the Raspberry Pi. This is a useful thing to try out any time that you have a project that doesn't really need a screen to get the work done.

- **Work with VNC to make another computer the remote screen:** If you need to access the Raspberry Pi remotely and you need to work with the graphical interface, then virtual network computing, or the VNC, is the best bet. You will then be able to see the desktop from the Raspberry device on your computer desktop and then control it as needed. This option is kind of slow, so you shouldn't use it all the time. But for occasional use to make things easier, it can be a great option. When you are at this point, you will know that you have a Raspberry Pi device that has all of the setup and configurations that you need ready to go. It should be all ready for you to start working with and using.

With all of this set up and ready to go, it is now time to move on to the next step. We will now spend some time learning more about the codes and the programming you can do with a Pi, so that you will be ready to use your new device to accomplish a variety of tasks.

Chapter Three: How to Use Raspberry Pi

As soon as you start up your Raspberry Pi after a fresh installation of the Raspbian OS, you'll encounter a first-time setup wizard. This is a really helpful tool that walks you through calibrating your Raspberry Pi system and allowing you to personalize some settings. This procedure is also known as the "configuration" of your Pi system.

1. As you progress through the setup procedure by clicking the *Next* button, you'll be prompted to specify your country, preferred language, and time zone. This helps the system to use the appropriate dictionary for your selected language, and characters on the screen will be displayed in the language you select. Once you set the time zone, the system will automatically update the date and time accordingly. If you look just below these drop-down lists, you'll see a box that specifies the *Use US keyboard* option. This option is for cases where you have been using the US layout keyboard regardless of the language you selected. Make sure Raspbian uses the correct keyboard layout. The other option, *Use English language*, basically sets the default language of the desktop and programs to be English regardless of the native language you have specified above.

2. After finishing setting up the country, language, and time zone, proceed by clicking *Next*. This will take you to the next window prompting you to set up a password for your user account to prevent any unauthorized login to your Raspberry Pi system.

3. When you have finished setting up a strong password, the configuration wizard will display a list of available Wi-Fi connections near you and ask you to connect to one. If you are planning to use a wired (Ethernet) connection instead of a wireless connection, then you can simply skip this part of the setup by clicking the *Skip* button.

4. The version of the OS installed from the NOOBS menu doesn't need to be up to date. If you have an older NOOBS version, then the OS will obviously not include its newer firmware updates. Hence, this configuration wizard gives you the option to check for system updates and install them if you are indeed running an older version of the OS. This is not a necessary step, but it is recommended to go through a system update check regardless because Raspbian is regularly updated to patch out and fix some system bugs, add new features to the OS, and improve system performance through optimization. Downloading the system update can take some time

based on how fast your internet connection is. When the updates have been downloaded and successfully installed, the system will display a window with the message *System is up to date*. Click the *OK* button and continue through the configuration.

5. This is the final screen of the setup wizard and prompts the user that, to wrap up and apply the specified configuration, the system requires a reboot. You can restart the system immediately or click the *Later* button to delay the system reboot. Once you have restarted the system and logged into the desktop by entering your password, you will not be prompted with the welcome wizard again, and the settings specified earlier will have been saved and applied to the system. Now, the Pi's software is ready to be explored.

Navigating Through the Desktop Interface

On the desktop interface, there are two icons placed by default, namely, the Wastebasket and the Removable Drive. These are the same as the Recycle Bin and ThisPC icons found on Microsoft Windows desktops. At the top, you'll see the Raspbian OS task bar, which allows the user to actually load programs that are then indicated as tasks in the task bar.

Going to the right-hand side of the task bar, you will find familiar icons, each representing features commonly found in every smart device nowadays. From left to right, we have:

1. The Media Eject icon

2. The Bluetooth icon

3. The Network icon

4. The Volume icon

5. The Clock icon

Going through the features of each of these icons from left to right, if you have a removable storage media connected to the Pi system, such as a USB flash drive, the Media Eject icon will display a selection of options, the main one being *Safely Eject and Remove Media Storage.*

Beside the Media Eject icon, you'll find the Network icon. This icon will change depending on the type of connection you're using. If you are connected to a wireless network, then you'll see a series of bars indicating the strength of the signal, and if you're connected to a wired network, you will just see two arrows. Clicking on the network icon will open up a drop-down menu showcasing all the available wireless connections and *Turn Off Wi-Fi* options.

Moving onwards is the Bluetooth icon; this icon will help you connect and pair with other Bluetooth devices such as wireless peripherals.

Next, the volume icon opens the volume mixer and gives access to the sound control panel. The clock icon displays a calendar and gives access to date and time options.

Going to the opposite side, the left-hand side of the task bar, you will find some useful launcher icons which give the user access to some commonly used features of the Raspberry Pi. From right to left, we have:

1. The Command Prompt launcher

2. The File Explorer launcher

3. The Web Browser launcher

4. The Menu launcher

The Menu launcher basically opens up a list showing where you'll find programs that are installed alongside Raspbian. Whenever you install a new program, it'll be added into its respective category in this menu launcher, from which you can quickly navigate and access the program. The other launchers are self-explanatory in their functions: the command prompt launcher opens up a Command Prompt window where you can directly instruct the system to perform actions, the File Explorer launcher opens up an explorer window in which you can go through the contents of your microSD card, and you can access the internet through the pre-installed Web Browser launcher. We will discuss the details of these programs in the next section.

The Chromium Web Browser

If you've ever used Google Chrome, the Chromium Web Browser will feel incredibly similar and easy to use. To open the Chromium Web Browser, simply open the menu launcher and position the mouse pointer over the *Internet* category. There, related programs will appear, and the Chromium Web Browser will be among them. Simply click on it to open it up.

To start using Chromium, make sure that you are connected to a wireless or wired internet connection and type in any website to start things off. For example, if you want to start surfing the internet, go to the Google Search engine. You can also maximize the Chromium window so that it occupies the maximum screen space available.

The Chromium window may also open up several web pages automatically on startup. These multiple web pages are displayed in separate tabs. To switch between web pages, you can click on their respective tabs. You may also access another tab by pressing the + icon beside any existing tabs, and can also close tabs by using the × icon.

The File Manager (Explorer)

Another name for File Explorer is File Manager. It is common to refer to this program by a variety of names, the most common ones being those mentioned above. In this program, you can explore and manage all of the files saved onto your storage media, regardless of if they are text files, programs, videos, images, web pages, or games; you can access every file and manage them through the File Manager.

The major function of the File Manager is to give the user access to directories (organized files and folders). You can access directories both on your microSD card and on any removable storage media (such as USB drives) that you connect to your Raspberry Pi. When you first open up the File Manager, the default window will be your home directory. In this directory, you'll find a series of subfolders known as subdirectories, which are arranged in categories just like the items in the menu launcher. The main subdirectories are:

1. **Desktop:** This folder is what you see when you first load Raspbian; if you save a file in here, it will appear on the Raspbian desktop, making it easy to find and load.

2. **Documents:** The Documents folder is home to most of the files you'll create.

3. **Downloads:** When you download a file from the internet using the Chromium web browser, it will be automatically saved in the Downloads folder.

4. **Music:** Any music you create or put on the Raspberry Pi can be stored here.

5. **Videos:** A folder for videos and the first place most video-playing programs will look.

6. **Pictures:** This folder is specifically for pictures, known in technical terms as image files.

7. **MagPi:** This folder contains an electronic copy of *The MagPi*, the official magazine of the Raspberry Pi Foundation.

8. **Public:** While most of your files are private, anything you put in Public will be available to other users of the Raspberry Pi, even if they have their own username and password.

Upon initial inspection, the File Manager is separated into two panes: an *easy access* pane on the left side, which shows the directories on the Raspberry Pi, and the *explorer pane* on the right side, which shows the subdirectories and files of the directory selected in the left pane.

You can also copy, delete, cut, and modify folders and files through the File Manager. For example, as soon as you plug in a

USB flash drive, a window will pop up asking if you want to display the contents of the removable drive in the File Manager. Clicking on the *Yes* button will open up a separate window of the File Manager, which will display all the contents (files and folders) of the removable drive; you can then copy, cut, delete, and edit these files and folders directly. Copying contents from a removable drive is also a very simple procedure. All you need to do is select the file or folder you want to copy, right-click on it, and a drop-down option will appear, from which you can find the *copy* function. Click on that, and the file will be copied onto the system's clipboard. Go to the directory where you want to copy the data, right-click on any empty space in the directory, and select the *paste* function.

When you've finished experimenting, close the File Manager by clicking the *close* button at the top-right corner of the window. If you have more than one window open, close them all. If you have connected a removable storage device to your Pi, eject it by clicking the eject button at the top right of the screen, finding it in the list, and clicking on it before unplugging it.

Shutting Down the Raspberry Pi

The most important skill to learn when using a Raspberry Pi is how to shut it down safely. All unsaved files are stored in the Raspberry Pi's volatile memory (memory that is emptied when the system is shut down). Therefore, you should get into the habit of securely shutting down the system to avoid losing crucial data.

Select *Shut Down* from the raspberry icon in the upper left corner of the desktop. A pop-up will appear with three options: *Shut Down*, *Reboot*, and *Log Out*.

Shut Down is the most common option; selecting it instructs Raspbian to close any open apps and files before shutting down the Pi. Wait a few seconds until the Pi's flashing green light goes off before turning off the power source.

Rebooting is essentially the same as shutting down the system, but instead of completely turning the system off, the system goes through a procedure of automatically starting up as soon as it finishes shutting down. Installation of some applications may prompt a system reboot; hence, you should properly restart the system instead of pulling out the power supply.

Log Out is useful in scenarios where there is more than one user account on the Raspberry Pi. To switch between user accounts or to turn off a user account without shutting down the system, you can choose the *Log Out* option. If you hit *Log Out* by mistake and want to get back in, simply type *pi* as the username and whatever password you chose in the Welcome Wizard at the start of this chapter.

Chapter Four: How to Program with Scratch

The idea behind using Raspberry Pi is not to use software developed by other people, but to use Raspberry Pi to create your own software based on your imagination. The Raspberry Pi is an excellent platform for you to create and experiment with programs on your own via a process known as *coding*.

Scratch Interface

Here are a couple of things to know before using the Scratch interface:

- **Sprite:** Sprites are the objects or characters that you control in a Scratch program, which sit on the *stage*.

- **Scripts Area:** This is the area where you drag and drop *blocks* from the *blocks palette* to build your program.

- **Stage Area:** Much like actors in a real-life play, the sprites that you create will be able to move around on the *stage area* as you control them via your program.

- **Sprites List:** Every sprite that you create or load into your Scratch program will appear in this part of the window.

- **Stage Controls:** Using *stage controls*, you can change your stage area to whatever you like, even if you want to include your own pictures as backgrounds.

- **Blocks:** *Blocks* are prewritten bits of program code that enable you to construct your program one step at a time.

- **Blocks Palette:** Every block in your program will show up in the *blocks palette* and also include color-coded categories.

Although it's a program designed for programmers aged eight and above, it's also accessible to younger programmers with a bit of guidance and help. It boasts a colorful and exciting interface and also features an impressive multimedia capability. That explains why most of the 5.5 million user-shared Scratch projects on the official website are games.

When kids are motivated to develop their own games, it's a great way to help them learn about coding and have fun at the same time. Also, thanks to the software's user-friendly interface and brilliant handling of core concepts, children are less likely to get bored, confused, or frustrated as they learn. Furthermore, the concepts children learn in Scratch provide a good base for progression when it comes to learning a more flexible language such as Python.

But Scratch offers a lot more than just being a framework for games. It can even be used to create interactive cartoons, presentations, and it interfaces with external motors and sensors using add-on hardware like the LEGO WeDo and PicoBoard robotics kit, or even straight through the Raspberry Pi's GPIO port.

I recommend that you get the Raspbian distribution of the Raspberry Pi, as it includes the latest preloaded version of the Scratch development environment. And if you're already following our suggestions within this book, then you're all set to go.

Hello World

Whenever someone starts to learn about programming, starting with a very basic program is tradition, especially when the program shows only one line of text. This program is commonly known as a *Hello World* program and is the first thing learners are acquainted with when creating their own programs.

Scratch, unlike a conventional programming language, doesn't require users to go through and memorize instruction names like inkey$ or print. Rather, most of the things they'll be doing are dragging and dropping blocks of code and then organizing them in a logical pattern.

You can start Scratch by double-clicking its icon located on the desktop, or by clicking on it in the *Programming* menu. The same principle is applied in a Scratch 2 interface. After that, the main Scratch interface will be displayed on your screen. If the screen appears small or off-centered, click the *Maximize* button to expand it.

There are multiple panes within the Scratch interface. To the left side is the *block palette*, which houses a variety of *code blocks* that enable users to develop their programs. A line of objects, known as *sprites*, can be viewed in the bottom right pane, as well as a control for the *stage* where the sprites show up. The stage appears in the window's top right side, which is where users can see the program running. The middle area of the window is where users can construct their program.

There's already a new Scratch project that comes with a blank page and a single sprite to help users get started. What it doesn't have at the moment is a program, so it won't do users any good to click the icon of a green flag that's at the top right corner of the window, because the software doesn't know what you want to do yet.

So first, you have to change the block palette, which is on the left side of the screen, to *Looks* by clicking the *Looks* button.

When you go a bit down the list of Looks blocks, you'll come across one that says *Hello!* All you have to do is click this with your left mouse button and drag it to the middle of the *Scripts* window. You can also click the block that is labelled *Hello!* If you want to go down the decades-old way of programming, you can customize it so that it says *Hello World!* If you want to delete blocks, click on a block using the right mouse button and then select *Delete* from the drop-down menu using the left mouse button.

The program still won't do anything if you click the green flag now. The reason why is because, despite Scratch knowing that it has to make the sprite say something, it doesn't know when to. Fortunately, you can do this with a *trigger block*, which you can find in the block palette's *Control* section.

By clicking *Control*, you can view this section and then drag the top entry that is labelled *when [flag icon] clicked* and place it just over the purple *Say* block. If you drop the piece close enough, it will automatically enter the existing brick, like a jigsaw piece.

The basis behind Scratch's concept is that several bricks are connected. When you take a look at the Control brick that you have recently placed, you'll find that there isn't a hole connecting at the top. If this is the case, then users are unable to stack another brick on top. And this is because the Control brick has been made to trigger several other bricks directly and has to happen at the start of a stack. But if you look at the bottom of the *Say* brick, you'll see that it has a connector that can fit into the top of any other brick, which means that you can place more bricks from underneath.

Animation and Sound

Although Hello World is quite basic, it's not exactly appealing. This is because it doesn't exactly show off Scratch's true power, which is what the sprite-handling system and multimedia functionalities are capable of. This system is equipped for simple animations, which can serve as the basis for an interactive game.

To get started, load a fresh new program in Scratch or click *New* from the *File* menu. You can start your new Scratch project with the default sprite, which is what you will be controlling.

You can use the block palette's *Motion* section to control simple Scratch animations. You'll always have a default palette when starting a new project. Click the box that says *move ten steps* and then drag it to the Scripts area. This block, as the name indicates, instructs the sprite you selected to move ten steps in the direction it faces. This default Scratch sprite will always face to the right directly—therefore, the *move ten steps* block will tell the sprite to move ten steps to the right.

You can change the value of the sprite's steps to anything other than ten. For example, if you change the value of the steps to 30, the block will be labelled *30 steps*. Though seeing an animated cat moving to the right isn't exciting, we suggest using the *Sound* block palette and dragging the block that says *play sound me out* to the Scripts area, and then linking it below the present *Move* block. If you want to keep the catlike sprite for a while, go to the Control block palette and choose *wait 1 sec*, or else the sprite will quickly flick between its starting point and target position.

If you want to make your animated cat run several times without vanishing off the edge of the stage, include another block labelled *move ten steps* below the block labelled *wait 1 sec* and then change it to *move -30 steps*. You can use negative figures like this, and Scratch won't mind. If your sprite can move a certain distance by adding the value of 30, -30 will have the character moving the same distance in the opposite direction.

Lastly, attach the block labelled *when [flag icon] clicked* from the Control block palette to the stack of blocks at the top of the Script area to finish the program. You can activate the program by clicking the green flag on the top right corner of the screen. If you want to hear sounds, connect your speakers or headphones to the Raspberry Pi.

You can also take this simple piece of animation in several other directions. Additional sprites can be created by clicking the *New Sprite* option underneath the stage on the right side of the window. These have the same capabilities as the first sprite, and can act independently. You can even add a thought bubble by changing the *Say* block from the first example to a *Think* block and make an animated comic strip.

What's even more fascinating is that this simple example teaches children essential programming concepts. In spite of being only five blocks long, this example covers sound playback, sprite movement in positive and negative distances, as well as the concept of *delays*. To try another concept—which might drive you up the wall due to its constant noises—try to add a *forever* block from the Control block palette. This brings a loop to your program, where it runs through the list forever—or at least until you hit the red stop button when your patience has reached its limit. The block can be dragged between *move 30 steps* and *when [flag icon] clicked* to include your existing blocks to the loop automatically without deleting them and starting over.

A Simple Game

You can take simple animation even further with Scratch by enabling the software to read inputs from your keyboard, thereby introducing interactivity. When you combine simple animation controls with the program above, you can create a simple game out of it, through the introduction of *if statements*, *sprite collision*, and *input*.

To do this, you'll need to start a new Scratch project—remember to save the previous example—and start by dragging the block labelled *move ten steps* to the Scripts area. But instead of telling the code blocks to execute when you click the flag icon, drag a block labelled *when space key pressed* above the blocks that say *move* by going to the Control block palette.

The block labelled *when space key pressed* is looking for the user's input, which, as the name suggests, is when the user presses the space key and uses that as the trigger for activating a list of blocks. You can execute the block at any time. By immediately pressing the spacebar, the sprite will do as instructed, which is moving ten steps to the right.

But let's be honest: having a character moving in only one direction doesn't sound like much fun at all, so you should click and drag a new *when space key pressed* block into the Scripts area. You won't be able to link this block to the existing list—you only have a single trigger block to work with—so it's best to start a new list anywhere down below. Like last time, you can customize the block using the down-arrow button that's located right next to the word *space* so that the block reads *when left arrow key pressed*. And then, change the block palette back to a motion palette and connect *move ten steps* under the new

43

block that says *when left arrow key pressed* before switching it to *move -10 steps.*

Since it makes more sense to use the left and right arrow keys, you can do the same thing with the original *when space key pressed* block; simply customize the block once more, using the down-arrow button, to change *space* to *right arrow key.* Now, you can move your cat in both left and right directions by pressing the left and right arrow keys. If you press the left arrow key, the cat will move ten steps left (but to Scratch, it is moving -10 steps to the right,) and if you press the right arrow key, the cat will move ten steps right.

With this, players will be able to move the sprite. But now it's time to instruct the sprite to do something. Seeing as how this is a very simple game, you should instruct your sprite to, let's say, pick up some food. To get started, go to the *File* button and click on the *Choose New Sprite* option, which you can find in the middle of the three buttons that are above the *Sprite* palette at the Scratch window's bottom right side. If you want to know which button is what, hover your mouse pointer over a button until they give you a pop-up tip.

After doing that, a message box will show, asking you to choose a sprite; double-click on the *Things* folder and double-click the *Cheesy Puffs* sprite. A new sprite will be placed in the sprite palette, which gives you a new object in the game to control.

Tip: The Scratch program is designed to be multithreaded and a bit object-oriented, meaning that every object in the program, like sprites, has its own code attached and that every code's section will run independently and simultaneously to other blocks. If you use the features right, you might also be able to create complex programs.

Any new sprite that is added to the scratch project appears right at the center on the stage by default, which leads to the existing cat sprite becoming obscured. To fix this dilemma, all you have to do is drag the new sprite with your left mouse button to the right.

You will find that the new cheesy puffs sprite is too large for your animated cat to eat. No problem! Just go to the top right side of the stage area and click the *Shrink Sprite* button, and you'll find four arrow keys that are pointing inwards. You can hover your mouse cursor over each pointer to find out which one is what.

When you click the *Shrink Sprite* button (or the *Gross Sprite* button, which does the complete opposite,) you will witness the mouse cursor becoming a replica of that button's icon. Then all you have to do is click the cheesy puffs sprite with the new cursor to shrink it. Keep clicking the cheesy puffs sprite until it is a decent size. After you're done, you can change the mouse cursor back to normal by clicking anywhere outside of the Stage area. Then drag the cheesy puffs sprite closer to the stage's right edge, if you like.

Now try moving your cat sprite toward the cheesy puffs sprite using the arrow keys on your keyboard. But, when you bring both sprites closer, nothing will happen. This is because the program hasn't been given instructions to take any specific action when sprites meet up with one another—also known as a *sprite collision*. This is where you introduce a new block known as a *Sensing* block.

Make sure that the cheesy puffs sprite is active (this is indicated when the image appears at the top of the Scripts pane, and if it doesn't, then just double-click the sprite on the stage) and then click the *Sensing* button to switch the Blocks palette to Sensing mode. Click and drag a *touching?* block from the Sensing palette to the Scripts pane.

The *touching?* block can be customized in the same manner as the *when space key pressed* block in order to control the cat sprite's movement. Choose *Sprite1* (cat sprite) from the list by clicking the down-arrow button located next to the question mark. When the two sprites meet up with each other, the block will activate.

Tip: You can also give your sprite a name by clicking on the box next to the sprite's image in the Scripts pane and typing whatever name you want. If you want, you can name the sprites specifically as "Cat" and "Cheesy Puffs," making it easier for you to keep track of the changes you make in the program.

If you look at the shape of the *touching Sprite1?* block, you will see that it doesn't have any jigsaw-like connectors at the top or the bottom and that it has a diamond shape, similar to a flowchart's decision point. That *is* no coincidence, as most of the Sensing blocks have to be embedded in a separate Control block for them to operate.

Change the blocks palette to Control mode and find the *if* block, which looks like a squished and bumpy letter *c*. You will notice that the *if* block has a similar diamond-shaped indentation as that of the *touching Sprite1?* block. Click and drag the *if* block into the Scripts pane and then click and drag the block labelled *touching Sprite1?* into the diamond-shaped indentation. You'll get a block of two colors that says *if touching Sprite1?* (or any other name that you decide to give the cat sprite).

This will be the program's *if conditional*. With this, every code within the domain will be executed only when the condition has been met. Here, the condition is when the cheesy puffs sprite is touched by the cat sprite. Using the *and, or,* and *not* logic blocks from the *Operators* block palette, you can create some complex scenarios.

Drag a *say Hello! For 2 secs* from the *Looks* block palette into the center of the *if touching Sprite1?* conditional. You can rewrite the text to make it say *Don't eat me!* and then include a *wait for 1 secs* Control block and change the value to 2. Then attach a *when space key pressed* block on the top, and change the value so that it says *when right arrow key pressed*. Lastly, click and drag a block labeled *hide* from the *Looks* palette to the bottom of the loop.

Return to editing the scripts by double-clicking the cat sprite on stage. The script that you made for the cheesy puffs sprite will go away. But don't worry, the script is still there in the background and will only appear when you're editing that sprite.

Boolean Logic

Boolean logic, or Boolean algebra—named after George Boole—is an essential concept to help users understand how computers work. Boolean logic can be implemented in three of Scratch's Operator bricks: *and*, *or*, and *not*.

The *and* operator requires two inputs (like Sensing blocks) to be true before its output can be true. The output will turn out to be false if any or both of its inputs are false; the output will only be true if both inputs are true. This operator can be used as an example to see if a sprite touches two other sprites.

For the *or* operator, either one or another of the two inputs have to be true. If any one of the inputs is true, then the output of the operator will be true as well—the convenient way to reuse code. For instance, if numerous sprites are harming the player sprite, only one block of code with the *or* operator can be used to trigger whenever any of the enemy sprites are being touched.

Lastly, the *not* operator is also referred to as an *inverter*, which means that its single output is the opposite of what its output is. This means that if the input is false, then the output is true. Similarly, if the input is true, then the output is false.

Click and drag another *if* block from the Control palette with a Sensing block that reads *touching?*, and change the Sensing block so that both of the blocks say *if touching Sprite2?* Insert a *wait 1 secs* Control block into this block, change the value to 2 and change a Looks block that reads *say Hello! for 2 secs* to *Yum-Yum-Yum!* Lastly, drag the entire stack of blocks up so that it connects to the bottom of the block that reads *when right arrow key pressed*, under the *move ten steps* block.

You can start your game by moving the animated cat sprite toward the cheesy puffs sprite using your keyboard's right arrow key. By the time the cat reaches the bowl of cheesy puffs, there will be a dialogue exchange, after which the bowl will disappear.

Even though this is a fine way to showcase important programming concepts, it's not exactly the best example of coding a game. Scratch features a *message broadcast* system that enables users to attach code to one object so that it communicates with the code attached to another object, creating neater collision results that don't necessarily rely on carefully timed causes.

You can try using the Control palette blocks labeled *broadcast* and *when I receive* to experiment with broadcasting. A message created for any object's broadcast block will trigger code with the *when I receive* flag, allowing you to link several objects and their code together.

Chapter Five: Writing Our Own Python Programs in the IDLE

Now that we have covered the basics of installing the operating system and had a chance to look at some of the fun things that we are able to do with the Pi device, it is time to get down to business and look at some of the great things that we are actually able to do with our new system.

In this chapter, we will introduce the Python programming language, learn how it works a bit, how to add it into the Pi device, and then start with some coding that will help us get the device to work in the manner that we want.

While there are many programmers who stick with Raspbian and use it as the chosen coding language to use on the Raspberry Pi, many beginners will find that working with the Python language is a lot easier.

Python is a really easy coding language to work with and is often the best option for those who have never spent any time learning code in the past. While there are a lot of reasons that we can enjoy the Python language, such as it being easy even for a beginner to learn how to use, and how to code in no time, it is also going to be strong enough to get the programs that we want done in a short amount of time. However, before you can go through and write out a program with the help of this language, we need to make sure that we are using the right IDLE editor on Pi so that it actually works.

So, to make this happen, one of the first steps is to download the IDLE editor for Python and then install it on our device. The IDLE is something that we are able to easily download right from the Python website. The IDLE is important for actually having a good environment to write out the codes we want, and stands for the Integrated Development and Learning Environment.

There are a lot of benefits that we are able to utilize not only with the Python language, but also when we actually work with the proper IDLE editor to write out the codes in Python. Once you are on the right web page to download the IDLE, you can then go through and choose which version of Python you would like to work with. Right now, we will pick from Python 2 or Python 3.

The differences are not much other than a few features, but most people decide that Python 3 is the best option to help them because it is the most recent version. There are a few instances when Python 2 will be the best one to work with, so do a bit of research and learn which is the best for your needs. After you have chosen which program to use, go ahead and download it onto your system and install it. You need to allow a few minutes to get the install done. You can then run the IDLE by finding it under the *applications* menu.

Once we have the IDLE running, keep in mind that we will then have two main methods to work with to write out Python programs in this editor. The first one is to write out the code in our console. The second one is to open up a new document, write out the whole program we want, save it, and then run the code when it is time to do so.

Both of these methods work, and professionals as well as beginners swear by both of them. Often the choice will depend more on the method that you like the best. When we enter into the next section, we will look at both of these examples and see which one is the most likely to work for your needs so you can make the right decision.

To make it simple, you will find that if your goal is to find a good way to test out a part of your code, or if you are working with a relatively small piece of code, then you want to write it out in the console to make things easier. But if you plan to work with a long piece of code and write out a big program, then you will want to work with the document instead.

Writing Code in Your Console

So, we will take a look at how we can write out some of the codes that we want to use right in the console. When we want to write out a small bit of code, then we will want to work with the console, and we have to enter it all going one row at a time.

Then, when we are done with the row, we can press the *Enter* button so that we end up on the next line.

When you work with this, and you start it out with the *def* keyword, the program will then recognize that we would like to write out a type of code that is known as a *function*. Once you have entered the function, which we will show the code for in a moment, you will then need to click on the *Enter* button so that you can go to the next line.

After you are done with that function and the command, you can then call it up with a *passing string argument*. To see how this will work, look at the code example that we have below:

>>>*def printString(text):*

print (text):

return

>>>*printString("Hello World"):*

Hello World

>>>

When you go through and type this into your editor, you will get the result of *Hello World* to show up on your screen. We will spend some time talking about functions a bit more in the next chapter, but this is a good introduction to help you get started.

Writing Code in a New Document

Writing out some simple codes that are only a few lines long, like what we did above, will be just fine to do within the console. You do not need to go through the same amount of work as we will look at in a moment just to write out a few lines of code overall.

But when we want to write out a whole program on the Raspberry Pi, then we need to make sure that we are able to handle some of the edits and more that may show up along the way, and working on it in a document that we are able to save is a better option.

When we would like to write out some of our programs in Python in a document, we will then be able to save the various parts that go with it. It is necessary in this case to get into the IDLE editor that we already installed earlier, and then we can go to the top left of our screen where the *File* is located. Then click on *New File* to continue on.

Then, you should see a new window pop up that you can work in. From here, the first thing that we need to do is save the file that we want to work with. You can either click on the file and then *Save* or just use the command CTRL+S.

After you have been able to save the file, you can paste the code that we used in the previous example into the new file. When the code is ready, you can run it by simply pressing the *Run* option and then clicking either the F5 key or *Run Model*. One thing to note here is that if your file isn't saved, the program will prompt us to save it. Once you decide to run the code, it will be executed in the Python Shell or the main window.

As you are able to see here, both of the methods for writing out your codes will be simple and easy to work with. This second option, though, will usually be the best one if you want to write out long codes and programs, because it is easier to save your work as you go and will ensure that if there is something that goes wrong with the computer or the system while you do the work, you will not lose all of that code in the process.

How to Write Python Comments

Before we end here, we need to look at another important component of writing codes in Python, whether you are doing it on your Raspberry Pi device or in another computer system.

This is a discussion on comments and how they work in this language.

There will be some situations when you are working on your codes, whether they are simple or advanced, and you will need to add in a little note about a particular part of the code. This could be a part where you need to name the code, tell yourself or another person a bit more about what you planned on doing in that part of the code, or even just leave a message of some sort.

However, even though you are leaving these little notes, you do not want them to come through and actually affect or slow down the program that you are writing out at the time. In order to write out one of these Python comments and get them to work without ruining the rest of your code, you need to use the # or hash character and then extend it to the end of the line.

You are able to use these comments either at the beginning of the line, or you can do it at the end when the rest of the code is done for that part. If you do this in the proper manner, you will find that you are able to write out these comments, and they will not make any changes to the code and the output that you get. In fact, when you write out the codes and execute them, the comments are not even seen or noticed when you run the program. They are just there as a point of clarification, not an important part of the code.

You do have the option to add in as many or as few of these comments as you would like based on your code. You could have these on every line of the code if you would like. The general rule here is that you do not want to go through and add in too many because it makes a big mess of the code and makes it harder to read through.

As we can see here, there are a lot of parts that come together when we work with the Python code. We need to make sure that we have the IDLE editor up and running and working on our Raspberry Pi to ensure that it will behave in the manner that we need to write codes. And then, we are able to go through and actually start writing some codes in Python to create the programs that we want.

Chapter Six: Simple Projects to Work Within Raspberry Pi

This guidebook has taken some time to explore a lot of the neat things that we are able to do when it comes to using the Raspberry Pi device. It is a simple start that helps us to learn more about programming and make small projects along the way.

With some of that behind us, though, it is time to dive right in and look at a few of the projects that we are able to create with Pi. There are a lot of projects that are possible when we work with the Raspberry Pi. In fact, this is a device that was designed to help beginners work through some of the tough starting steps of programming and coding, so the ability to create lots of projects was a must.

Some of the different projects that we are able to explore when it comes to working with the Raspberry Pi device include the arcade box, and turning the Raspberry Pi into a phone. We'll cover both in turn in this chapter.

The Arcade Box

The first kind of project that we want to take a look at is how we are able to take the Raspberry Pi device and turn it into our own little arcade box so we can play games and more.

This will give us a little bit of practice with what we are able to do with this device, and you will find that the Raspberry Pi is a good controller to use to make an arcade box because it has the potential to hold onto a lot of games, especially if you utilize various SD cards.

Before we do that, though, there are a number of steps that the programmer has to accomplish in order to make this all happen. We need to also make sure that we have all of the necessary tools and accessories in place to really make our own arcade box. Some of the different supplies and options that we need to keep around when creating our own arcade box will include:

- A game controller is not necessary, but it can make playing some of the games a little bit easier.

- A power supply so that the device turns on.

- The Raspberry Pi 3 (or other Raspberry Pi device that you want to use).

- A good SD card (this card needs to be at least 4GB in order to make the games work).

- An HDMI cable to hook your device up to a monitor.

- A TV.

The first step is to get the games from the RetroPie website over to your Pi. We are going with the RetroPie website to help us get some of the older games that we will use for this device. You will simply need to download the website onto your SD card, and then put them on the Pi device. To do this, visit the RetroPie website's Download page, and from there, you are able to pick out the version of the Raspberry device that you want to work with. Give it some time to copy over to your SD card.

Once everything is over on the SD card, you can turn on the Raspberry device. Add in the controller and plug the device into the television while you wait for it to load up. Add the SD card into the device and give it a few minutes to boot up.

If you did the conversion properly, then you should see the EmulationStation come up on the television screen. As we start to work on this step and we get something to show up on the screen, we can then go through and make sure that any and all of the configurations that are necessary here are complete. The controller is often the best way to handle this because it can make it easier to navigate menus. With the controller, we can just go through and click on only the things that we need before finishing it all up.

The first time that we do this will take a bit of time because we have never done it before, but the more times we have to go through it, the faster the project will go. After we have been able to go through and get the Wi-Fi hooked up and ready to go to our device, and you are certain that you have gotten it started up and ready to go, then it is time to add on the ROMs part to this device as well.

Getting this set up and running will take a few moments, but the process is simple and pretty similar to what we did before. To do this, we either need to make sure that we have a nice strong internet connection, or we can use an Ethernet cord. If your connection is not strong and the ROMs get interrupted, then you will end up with some messy problems to try and fix.

Go onto your main computer. If you are using a Windows computer, you can open up the file manager on the computer and type in a simple code of *//retropie*. If you are working with a Mac computer, you can go to the *Finder* window, select *Go*, and then click on *Connect to Server*. You would then type in the code *smb://retropie*. Both of these end up with the same results—they just have to be done a bit differently on different computers.

At this point, we should have the Wi-Fi and other parts connected properly, and that is when we will be able to move the ROMs onto our device. We should do this remotely, meaning we will use the SD card to move our chosen games over, or we can choose which games we will use the most often and put those directly on the Raspberry Pi device. When you have them transferred through either method, then it is time to start playing!

Turning the Device into a Phone

The second project we can do is to turn our Raspberry Pi device into a phone. This is actually easier to do than it may seem, though we have to keep in mind that it will not be the most advanced phone. We will not be creating a phone like a smartphone or anything like that, but it will be able to send and receive calls and even do some basic texting, which can be pretty cool. To get started with this one, we need to make sure that we have the right tools, and those include:

- Headphones

- Microphone

- An electrical switch

- Velcro squares to help hook it all together

- A touch screen

- A GSM module that has an antenna and some audio outlets

- A battery pack to help power the phone

- A Raspberry Pi 3 that can handle the Python coding language

- Duct tape

- Cables

- Zip ties

- A SIM card

- A converter for DC-DC

- A foam board that you are able to cut down to be the same size as the Raspberry Pi

When you are picking out the supplies that you need for this project, you should double-check that they will be compatible with the Pi 3 and not one of the other versions of Raspberry Pi. There are a lot of choices out there in terms of the supplies that you can use, and many of them come at a lower price. But you want to make sure that they are of high enough quality and that they actually will work with the device that you want to use.

After we make sure that we have all of the right supplies that will work with our Raspberry Pi device, it is time to put the software we need on the device as well. For this to work, we need to bring in that Python that we talked about earlier, so make sure that this language has been added to our Raspberry Pi device as well. While we are in this process, we need to make sure that we add on a few other types of software as well, including the PiPhone and the WireHunt, so that it will be easier to turn this simple board into the phone that we want to use. The easiest way for us to add these pieces of software to our device is to add them to the SD card first and then just transfer those over one at a time.

Now that all of these items are present and ready to go, it is time for us to start turning the device into a phone. The first step to doing this is to connect our battery so that the board, or our phone, will be able to start up. We need to do this over a switch, so the battery ends up with the necessary power.

Once we have this done, it is time to hook both of these to the GSM module. Take the header of the GSM and then connect it over to the converter that you are using.

Once we have connected all of these together, it is now time to hook them up to the Raspberry Pi device. We can do this with some of the other cables that you should have. The first part of all of this is to connect the device with the other transmit pins to ensure that they will stay with one another. Check that the pins are all connected to the T and the Rx ports. While this will require us to connect quite a few parts together, once we get this done, and can work with the SIM card, then we are good to go.

Now that all of our lines have been connected and our SIM card is in place, it is now time for us to actually assemble all of the parts. To make sure that this will work, we need to bring out that piece of foam and slice it to be the same size as our Pi device. Place the device over this piece of foam and then use the squares of Velcro and some duct tape to secure the two parts together.

This step is important because it will help us to connect the converter, the switch, and the module to the other side of our piece of foam. You have to make sure that when you add the battery pack that it goes to a place that is safe, usually somewhere between the Pi device and the screen. You do not want to have it so that the battery pack will move around and cause trouble. If it moves around, then the phone will turn off randomly or have issues along the way.

At this point, if all of the parts are connected in the proper manner, then you should notice that our phone will be done for the most part, and you should be able to turn it on and get it to actually work. To turn on the phone, you can just turn on the switch that goes to it.

From here, you can wait for it to turn on and boot up before calling any number that you want! As you can imagine, this will be a pretty simple kind of phone to work with.

The neat thing is that we can take this a bit further if we would like. For this project, we are just keeping it simple with a phone that can make and receive calls. But it is possible to take this simple phone and set it up to do some other options, like texting, even getting online, and so much more.

Final Words

Anyone can use Raspberry Pi to build amazing projects like retro games, robots, their own operating system, and so on. This book has helped you learn the basics of this. With the help of a Raspberry Pi, you can easily control a computer, or set up your own devices by connecting circuits and wires directly to GPIO pins.

We started this book by discussing the simplest of concepts and learned the details of the hardware components of the Raspberry Pi. After laying a foundation to understanding how similar the Raspberry Pi system is to a traditional desktop PC, we learned how to set up our Raspberry Pi's hardware and installed our first OS on it.

After getting to know the ins and outs of the Raspberry Pi's hardware and software, we were ready to take the next step in the world of computers and learned the basics of programming. We learned about the Pi's visual and interactive Scratch programming language and also introduced today's popular Python programming language so that we can benefit from the best of both worlds.

Then we ended the journey of learning about the Raspberry Pi by finishing off with the world of physical computing and delving into its basics whilst incorporating the newly learned knowledge in a few interactive examples.

I hope you found this beginner's guide helpful in getting started with the Raspberry Pi. The possibilities with the Pi are near infinite, as you will soon discover through your own practice. Finally, I hope you have an amazing time learning to code and create your own awesome Raspberry Pi projects to share with the world!

References

1. Arfeen, Ibrahim Eikhier Hussein, and Suliman, Abd Elrazig Awadelseed Edries. "Real-Time Monitoring for Data Greenhouse Based on Raspberry Pi Technology." *Open Access Library Journal* 6 no. 3 (March 2019): 1–8.

2. Gonzalez-Huitron, Victor Alejandro, León-Borges, José Antonio, Rodriguez-Mata, Abraham Efraim, Amabilis-Sosa, Leonel Ernesto, Ramírez-Pereda, Blenda, and Rodriguez Rangel, Hector. "Disease Detection in Tomato Leaves Via CNN with Lightweight Architectures Implemented in Raspberry Pi 4." *Computers and Electronics in Agriculture* 181, no. 7 (February 2021).

3. Jolles, Jolle W. "Broad-Scale Applications of the Raspberry Pi: A Review and Guide for Biologists." *Methods in Ecology and Evolution* (June 2021): 1–18.

4. Kadhar, Mohaideen Abdul K., and Anand, G. "Basics of Python Programming." In *Data Science with Raspberry Pi.* (Berkely, CA: Apress, 2021), 13–47.

5. Korber, Nina, Geldreich, Katharina, Stahlbauer, Andreas, and Fraser, Gordon. "Finding Anomalies in Scratch Assignments." Conference paper from the 2021 IEEE/ACM 43rd International Conference on Software Engineering: Software Engineering Education and Training (ICSE-SEET), May 2021. IEEE: 171–182.

6. Kroustalli, Chrysoula, and Xinogalos, Stelios. "Studying the Effects of Teaching Programming to Lower Secondary School Students with a Serious Game: A Case Study with Python and CodeCombat." *Education and Information Technologies*. (May 2021): 1–27.

7. Kurniawan, Agus. *Raspbian OS Programming with the Raspberry Pi*. (Berkeley, CA: Apress, 2019.

8. Martínez, Alexuan, Nieves, Christian, and Rúa, Armando. "Implementing Raspberry Pi 3 and Python in the Physics Laboratory." *The Physics Teacher* 59, no. 2 (February 2021): 134–135.

9. McManus, Sean, and Cook, Mike. *Raspberry Pi for Dummies*. New York: John Wiley & Sons, 2017.

10. McShane, Jack, Douglas, Mandy, and Meehan, Kevni. "Using a Raspberry Pi to Prevent an Intoxicated Driver from Operating a Motor Vehicle." Conference paper from the 2021 IEEE 11th Annual Computing and Communication Workshop and Conference (CCWC), January 2021. IEEE: 1023–1028.

11. Nagrath, Preeti, Jain, Rachna, Madan, Agam, Arora, Rohan, Kataria, Piyush, and Hemanth, Jude D. "SSDMNV2: A Real Time DNN-Based Face Mask Detection System Using Single Shot Multibox Detector and MobileNetV2." *Sustainable cities and society* 66, no. 6789 (December 2020).

12. Pankov, Pavel, Nikiforov, Igor, and Zhang, Yifeng. "Hardware and Software System for Collection, Storage and Visualization Meteorological Data from a Weather Stand." In Voinov, N. Shreck, T., and Khan, S. (eds.) Proceedings of International Scientific Conference on Telecommunications, Computing and Control, April 29, 2021. *Systems and Proceedings*, vol. 220. Springer, Singapore: 37–48.

13. Richardson, Matt, and Wallace, Shawn. *Getting Started with Raspberry Pi*. Sebastopol, CA: O'Reilly Media, 2012.

14. Suehle, Ruth, and Callaway, Tom. *Raspberry Pi Hacks: Tips & Tools for Making Things with the Inexpensive Linux Computer*. Sebastopol, CA: O'Reilly Media, 2013.

15. Wilkinson, Matthew, Bell, Michael C., and Morison, James I. L. "A Raspberry Pi-Based Camera System and Image Processing Procedure for Low Cost and Long-Term Monitoring of Forest Canopy Dynamics." *Methods in Ecology and Evolution* 12 (April 2021): 1316–1322.

16. Zhang, He, Srinivasan, Ravi, and Ganesan, Vikram. "Low Cost, Multi-Pollutant Sensing System Using Raspberry Pi for Indoor Air Quality Monitoring." *Sustainability* 13, no. 1 (January 2021): 370.

17. Halfacree, G. (2018). Using Your Raspberry Pi. In *The official Raspberry Pi Beginner's Guide: How to use your*

new computer (3rd ed., pp. 38–38). story, Raspberry Pi Press.

www.ingramcontent.com/pod-product-compliance
Lightning Source LLC
LaVergne TN
LVHW052311060326
832902LV00021B/3824

* 9 7 8 1 9 6 0 7 4 8 3 8 6 *